SUMMARY OF
BECOMING

BY

MICHELLE OBAMA

**Proudly Brought To You By
BOOK ADDICT**

WITH KEY POINTS
&
KEY TAKE AWAY

Disclaimer

This book is a summary and meant to be a great companionship to the original book or to simply help you get the gist of the original book. If you're looking for the original book, kindly go to Amazon website, and search for Becoming by Michelle Obama.

TABLE OF CONTENTS

EXECUTIVE SUMMARY

Before anything, you're going to want to read this because it shows just how much everyone -- regardless of position or title, race or color – is human. The former First Lady of the United States of America, Michelle Obama, is no different.

Becoming tells a tale of a young girl born in Chicago and takes us through her growing and formative years. It tells of how a woman found her voice in a discriminatory society; how she emerged strong, fearless, and confident.

Are you lost and wondering how to journey through life? This book is for you. Through every page and chapter, Michelle Obama speaks to your heart and soul, relaying her life and helping you live your best life! She shares her ups and downs, woes and successes, as a single lady, in marriage and even in her career.

Michelle takes the reader through what it's like to go from humble beginnings to occupying one of the most revered positions in the world: the struggles, the perks, and the achievements. She also opens up on feelings and thoughts about the current American president, Donald Trump.

Details in this book reveal many of our innermost fears and weaknesses, and show us how to look past them, plunging ahead for a greater tomorrow.

If you're ready to be blown away, and confronted with the very truths that you need to set your life in motion, then you should read this.

PART I: BECOMING ME
CHAPTER 1

Key Takeaways

- *I was a girl, in my own world.*
- *My family was home to me.*
- *Music ran in the family, and I learned to play the piano early on in life.*

As a young, growing child, I spent a lot of my years listening to unprofessional music, as they found their way through into my bedroom, from my great-aunt's apartment just below ours. My family resided in a tiny house in Chicago, belonging to my great-aunt, Robbie and her husband, Terry. I have always believed that my great-aunt Terry was rather terrific. In our community, she was the resident piano teacher. She also conducted the choir at a local church. I would hear children who took piano lessons continuously work on a particular song, trying so hard to get approval from great-auntie Robbie, who was very difficult to please. Worse still, they could only work one song per time. I was not irritated by the songs, but the diligence did get to me, as they would sing on and on. My only relief from this never-ending cycle was my father returning home from an early shift, where he'll put the Cubs game on TV, in such a manner that it would be loud enough to drain out all of the sound coming from under our apartment.

The Cubs were no bad a team to behold. They were not particularly fantastic either. My father would tell tales of how well the Cubs were playing, and what season of games we were in. In all of these, however, America was experiencing a huge change. The 1960s had voices like the Kennedy's, Martin Luther King Jnr, and a host of others silenced through death. In 1968, the democratic national convention went south, becoming bloody, causing many whites to relocate from the city.

I was, at this point, in a world of my own, too young to understand the things going on around me. Besides playing with barbies and blocks, I had no cares in the world. With my parents and my elder brother, I had the best of love and life. Early on in life, I learned to read, with my mother accompanying me to the public library where I read out loud from the pages of books. My father, a city laborer, worked during the day but returned at night to expose us to a life of art and music. A sports lover, he emptied his wallets to see my brother play basketball when Craig expressed his interest in the sport.

My elder brother, Craig, has always been my right-hand man. Incredibly supportive and protective, Craig took on a position of vigilance for, and responsibility to me, very early in his life. All these traits he demonstrated in a family picture which we took when I was about eight months old. At this point, my family found our home living across my grandparents' home in Parkway Gardens. Shortly after, however, my parents took up an offer to move into great-aunty Robbie and Uncle Terry's place, perhaps persuaded that it was a nicer neighborhood to live in. Our apartment was quite small, yet we all found a way to fit in there. My great-aunt's apartment, right below ours felt like some sacred museum, such that I began to imagine that two different worlds existed, upstairs and downstairs. Upstairs, Craig and I were ourselves, playful, noisy and carefree. It was another story entirely downstairs. Perhaps this was because my great-aunt and her husband were much older, having been born in a different age and time from even my parents, talk more of Craig and mine. At the time, my mother used to say that everyone on earth was moving about with some luggage of history. As the days passed, I learned that authorities once discriminated against my great-aunt when she registered for a choral music workshop in North-western University; she was denied a room in the women's residence. Instead, she was asked to make her residence somewhere in town, a place set apart for blacks. Her husband, Terry, used to have one of the finest jobs on the train then; moving luggage, serving meals and ensuring that passengers' welfare was adequately taken care of. For some weird reason, however, Terry never seemed to get past this way of life. He still dressed as smart as he did back in the days, with his suspenders and wing-tips screaming impeccable. Once every month, Terry would let himself loose, having just one cigarette and a cocktail. However, unlike my parents, he never unwound. A part of me secretly wished he'd speak, as I imagined him to have tons of tales about the cities he'd been to, and how rich people behaved on the train. Still, he never mentioned a thing.

I decided I'd learn to play the piano at about four years old. My very first lesson with my great-aunt Robbie had my legs hanging from the piano bench, as we began the lessons. And although it felt like a tough one when I started, I soon came to love the piano. I come from a family of musicians, particularly from my maternal side. However, at the crux of music in my family lay my grandfather, who was also great-aunt Robbie's brother. My grandfather had been separated from my grandmother tons of years before I was born when my mother was a teenager. He lived in our neighborhood, and had stereo equipment everywhere in the house, the bathroom inclusive. He didn't trust the world in so many ways, and thus, music seemed the perfect escape from all his worries.

I continued to focus on my piano lessons, quickly picking up the scales and getting fully immersed in sight reading. As I owned no piano of my own, I had to continue practicing downstairs at great-aunt Robbie's. I would often drag my mom along with me so she could hear me play. I would not say I was better than any of great-aunt Robbie's students, but I was indeed excited at the thought of learning. And sometimes, I would notice how pleased Great-aunt Robbie was, knowing that I had just played a song without a mistake, striking the right chords, and picking out melodies.

Great-aunt Robbie and I soon had a fallout as I, in my quest for more decided to go playing more technical songs in the lesson book. Thinking I had done something impressive, she crushed me, as she did many of her students, telling me that was not how to do things. I was surprised she was upset at me for wanting to discover something new, but she insisted that I could not learn the piano that way. And so, we kept going back and forth, week after week, neither of us willing to back down from our lofty heights. To my parents and Craig however, this was an entire comedy scene, as they laughed it all off.

Once every year, Great-aunt Robbie had a recital on Michigan Avenue. My father, on the one hand, loved to drive. My father's car provided some bonding for our family. It took me years to fully understand what it meant to my dad. He had been diagnosed with a painful leg condition which titled towards being immobile. As I sat to play my song at the recital, I was overtaken with fear and panic. Because I was used to playing my great-aunt's worn out piano, playing from a correctly-strung, neatly arranged piano seemed an impossible task. Aware of the faces looking at me, I tried to hide my fear. Great-aunt Robbie saw through all of these as she gently came up, placed my hand on the Middle 'C', and gave me all I needed to go on and make music.

CHAPTER 2

Key Takeaways

- *School was a love for me, not a bore.*
- *I kept to myself most of the time.*
- *My mother paid attention to every detail.*
- *Our world was simple: we made friends based on who wanted to play, and not by the color of our skins.*

I began kindergarten classes in 1969, armed with the knowledge of reading basic words, as well as having Craig, whom everyone seemed to take a liking to, ahead of me. The school was not far from home at all, as it was barely a two-minute walk or a one minute-run from the house, as Craig would do it. I fell in love with school right from the very first day. I liked my teacher as well. Quickly, I made friends with my classmates. Even as a little girl, I was assured of my reading prowess. You cannot begin to imagine how good I felt when I found out that our very first task would be learning new sets of words, by sight. The words we were to study were colors. One at a time, we took turns to read these words out loud. Quietly, I watched each child try so hard to pronounce the words boldly written on large manila cards, succeeding and stumbling at different points. One could notice how bad kids felt when they did not make it past 'red.' A smart kid was usually rewarded in school, and this has a way of boosting their confidence. In my class then, Chiaka and Teddy were the brightest of us all, and it remained that way for a long time.

I struggled to keep up with the duo. Upon getting to my turn, I would read out the easy words with little to no effort. Then came the tough ones like purple and orange, which took some time to pronounce. However, I lost it when I had to pronounce colors such as "White." I didn't realize it was "White" until I had been told to return to my seat. As I lay in bed that night, I spelled it back and forth, beating myself up over and over for failing to realize what the word was. I just hated the sting of embarrassment that came with being unable to pronounce these words correctly. Determined to do this right, when I returned to school the next day, I asked my teacher for a do-over. Initially, she disagreed, but I insisted. Finally, she let me have my way, and I went over all the colors, successfully pronouncing every one of them. Impressed with me, my teacher stuck a gold-foil star on my shirt as a sign of achievement, the same one she had stuck on Chiaka and Teddy's shirts the day before.

Back at home, I was in a world of my own with my dolls. Only on rare occasions would I choose to join other kids in the neighborhood who played outside after school. Similarly, I did not invite my school friends to my home. I liked my space, and I did not want anyone messing with my dolls. From my bedroom window though, I had a glimpse of the real world. I'd watch people and families go about their daily lives from the tiny corner of my room. We lived in a middle-class neighborhood, where kids made friends based on who was available to play and not by their skin color. I had three friends at the time, Rachel, Susie, and the Mendozas' grand-daughter. I was a kid then, unaware of the changes that were taking place around me. Fifteen years before my parents moved away from here, the neighborhood was predominantly white. By the time I was leaving for college, however, it had become mostly black.

It was in the midst of these that Craig and I were raised. We had Jewish, white and black families as neighbors. They all paid my great-aunt Robbie to teach their kids to play the piano. Of all the families in the community, my family could be considered poor; we knew our home wasn't ours. Unlike other neighborhoods, ours had not transitioned into one occupied by the not-so-better-off mass of the population. Soon after, however, we began to feel its effect too, particularly at school. We felt greatly the absence of a teacher who could effectively control her class, and particularly loved her students. The classrooms became disorganized and the students became disorderly. Our new teacher thought we were the worst set of kids she had ever seen, not realizing that much of it was her making because she was unable to structure and organize her class. Every day in class was long and boring, and I could barely wait for the lunch break when I could go home and pour my heart out to my mother. Understanding my distress, my mother went to my school, visited the appropriate quarters, made me write some tests all of which resulted in a promotion; I got moved up to a third-grade class overseen by a teacher who knew her stuff! And although this move seems insignificant, it did change a lot for me. At the time, I wasn't bothered about the kids who remained with the former teacher that could barely teach. But, today, I realize that even children know when they are undervalued and can express their anger in the form of disorderliness.

As the days went by, my mother would push me to go on out and play with the other neighborhood kids. She hoped I would be like my brother who seemed to have it easy, making friends with people everywhere he went. My brother, through his basketball game, seemed to get a lot of things done. He learnt to approach strangers, to talk, and also to demystify myths that existed about persons and neighborhoods around us. At age ten, I finally crawled out of my shell, venturing out into the open. Together with my brother Craig, I went on a bus to Lake Michigan every day, to return home by four. I lost interest in my dolls, and the apartment became hotter each afternoon, except when the air conditioner was working. Behind our house was Euclid Parkway, a community hosting about fifteen homes. This was paradise. However, before I would successfully make my way through to girls my age, I was always challenged by a girl named DeeDee, who often sat next to a more popular girl named Deneen. Deneen was a friendly person, but for some unknown reason, DeeDee did not seem to like me. She acted as though my mere presence was a party pooper.

Before long, I began to lose confidence in myself. At this point, I was aware of the choices that I had. I could decide to remain the new girl DeeDee took pleasure in tormenting, or I could return home to my dolls. I had a third option: I could earn her respect. The next time she tried getting at me, I hurled at her and threw a punch. I'm not sure now who it was that tried to pull us apart, but we were already rolling in the dirt and tugging at each other. That singular event signaled my welcome into the neighborhood tribe. DeeDee and I were perhaps destined never to be friends, but I had at least earned her respect.

Our once-bustling neighborhood soon began to lose its vibe, as most of those we grew to know and love started to relocate, making new homes in the suburbs. Worst hit of us all was my mother whose friend, Velma Stewart, suddenly told her that she would be moving alongside her family to a suburb called Park Forest. Soon after they moved, they invited my family over for a visit. We all went, and we were pretty disappointed that anyone would give up the fun, bubbly life they lived in Euclid for this far-off, quiet and uncrowded area. Soon enough, we arrived at the Stewarts' house, with my parents playing catch-up while my brother had an exciting day playing ball. Evening came, and we decided it was time to leave, only for us to realize that someone had scratched the side of my father's beloved Buick; it was a deliberate action, probably done with a stone or a key. My father, being someone who barely ever complained, got into the car, and drove us all home in silence. Soon enough, he was able to visit the body shop, where he had the scratch erased.

CHAPTER 3

Key Takeaways

- *Craig suddenly became our superman.*
- *I began to loosen up.*
- *Sunday afternoons- perfect afternoons!*

My ever-sweet brother Craig suddenly grew afraid of his surroundings, fretting and being more careful than usual. He became concerned that he might go blind or deaf or get amputated, causing him to acquire skills that would enable him to adapt if he found himself in any of these conditions. His greatest fear, however, was fire. House fires regularly occurred in Chicago, owing to different reasons. In fact, my grandfather moved into our neighborhood after his former house was razed down by a fire incident. I had also recently lost one of my classmates, along with two of his siblings in a fire incident that trapped them in their home.

Days went by, and Craig grew worse as his anxieties deepened. He took it upon himself to ensure that our family was safe at all times. We prepared against the strangest of things, worried greatly about our father's disability and inability to make it out in a hurry should an emergency occur. My father, on the one hand, did his best to be there for us all, despite his advancing multiple sclerosis, which weakened him by the day. He enjoyed his job and tried to make the best out of it.

Gradually, I began to loosen up, getting ready to take on the world. My frequent visits with my father drastically changed my outlook about people and the world generally. My mother had six siblings, while my father was the first child out of five. This explained why I had a ton of uncles and aunts, and numerous cousins as well. My maternal grandfather seemed to be the magnet that held the family together, often having everyone come over to enjoy his delicious meals. My father's family, however, lived not so close to us. My father was not a judgmental person, as he made friends with everyone-black or white, rich or poor. He loved and adored his family members, regardless of their lifestyle or financial status.

Sunday afternoons were great times for us all, because we would ride down to my grandparents' for dinner with them and my dad's three youngest siblings. To me, my father appeared more like a 'father' to them, as opposed to the elder brother he was. That aside, I found my uncles and aunt pretty cool. They seemed to always know what was in vogue. They wore trendy clothes and Craig and I could not help but spend time with them to learn of their 'freshness.' My grandfather was not particularly fun to be around, as he usually busied himself with a cigarette and newspaper; he complained about everything. My grandmother was his direct opposite however. She was a devout Christian, who found a way to take all of my grandfather's insults and complaints without mentioning a word in defense of herself. This, I found very annoying, so much that my mother once said that I was the only one who ever spoke back at my grandfather whenever he yelled. I loved my grandfather, no doubt, but I was irritated at the way he often yelled at my grandmother. Worse still, she never spoke up for herself. In most cases, I would ask him why he was mad or why he shouted at my grandma, to which he never replied, but instead, casually returned to his newspaper.

Perhaps the questions I hurled at my grandfather were rather tough and unanswerable; I would never know. Soon after though, I began to realize that, life itself had a lot of unanswerable questions.

CHAPTER 4

Key Takeaways

- *I spent my break at home, with my mother, every day.*
- *My school was fast losing its standard.*
- *My body was changing- I was growing!*

Every day at school, we had an hour to go on break. Since my home was not too far off and I had a mother who did not work, I jollied home in the company of some female friends, ready to eat my mother's sandwiches. This helped me form a habit that stuck throughout my life- having few, reasonable, female friends. Among ourselves, we talked about everything that happened at school. My mother was always excited to serve us, as it allowed her an entrance into what our tiny minds were harboring. She listened to our everyday gossip while she went about her daily chores.

The racial and economic crunch had begun, and my school, Bryn Mawr, went from good to bad. As more whites left the neighborhood, the school became more and more populated with poor, black students. My mother refused to be affected by any of these, but held on strongly to what she knew while controlling what she could. She soon became one of the most active PTA members at Bryn Mawr, helping out in more ways than one. She assisted greatly in ensuring the creation of a special multi-grade classroom, which was premised on having students grouped according to their abilities, rather than their ages. This was birthed by Dr.Lavizzo, Bryn Mawr's principal, who had recently gotten a Ph.D. in Education and had studied the new trend. As expected, the idea generated a lot of opposition. In some places around the country, however, it was gaining momentum. And for this reason, I spent my last three years as a student of Bryn Mawr, in a classroom apart from the rest of the school.

I shared everything with my mom. For some reason, I forgot to ask how she fared, or how she was comfortable being at home, and not working like a lot of other mothers. I only enjoyed the fact that there would always be food at home for me and my friends, and that my mother would usually volunteer to accompany my class, whenever we had to go, on an excursion. We had a spending limit at home, yet my mother never mentioned it. She did a lot of things for and by herself, being very creative and rather prudent in her dealings and spending. As a parent, she was brilliant and worthy of emulation. She was as humble as a dove, always willing to share in our joys and sorrows. She told us the truth all the time, the situation notwithstanding. My mother loved us, yet she did not spoil us. She taught us to be adults early on in our lives, so much so that she allowed us to make our own decisions, confident enough that we'd choose right.

By age fourteen, I considered myself a half-grown woman, coupled with the fact that I had begun menstruating, and my bra size had changed as well. I also had a new set of best friends -- the Gore sisters, who doubled as ideals for me. Diana, Pam, and their little sister, Gina were my definition of what being feminine entailed. They rarely spoke about their father. Their mother, Mrs. Gore, was an idol to behold with the best of makeup and perfumes; things my mother would consider exotic. Boys were not allowed into their home, even though they often came around the Gore house, in droves.

Like most girls, I became aware of the changes in my body pretty early. Now, I moved around my neighborhood much more independently, went on the bus on my own and ran errands for my parents, all by myself. I had learnt never to respond to boys who called at me while clustered on a street corner, knowing where or where not to go and so much more. Our parents were also fully aware that their kids had become teenagers, and therefore made a lot of changes at home in respect to this development. They created actual bedrooms for Craig and I and gave us phone extensions.

I gradually began to learn to be around boys, and slowly, I was getting separated from my parents. And like I was unbothered knowing how my mother fared being a full-time housewife, I cared less about what it meant to be married. My mother once told me that she sometimes had thoughts about leaving my father. I am not sure whether or not these thoughts were serious, but I can today say that even the sweetest of marriages have their challenges and that it is a union that requires renewal, over and over again.

CHAPTER 5

Key Takeaways

- *My mother returns to work.*
- *Chicago was much bigger than I thought.*
- *Princeton University beckons!*

At about the time I began high school, my mom did return to work, as an executive assistant at a bank. Like every other working-class person, she had a wardrobe full of work-clothes and began catching the bus to work. On certain occasions, she would ride along with my father in his precious Buick, when start times happened to line up. The job a much-needed development, as it helped the family's finances. Craig was already contemplating going to college, and I was right after him.

Craig had become a full grown man, viewed as one of the city's finest basketball players. He remained his ever beautiful self, simple and focused as he scaled the ladder in his athletic journey while maintaining excellent grades as a student. To avoid losing focus, my parents ensured that Craig attended the Catholic high school, which was rather expensive at the time.

Nevertheless, for him to have access to a great basketball team, and still be taught under a rigorous curriculum, they paid his tuition. It was not long before college teams began courting him. Once again, my parents told him to keep all his options open, and remain focused on getting admitted into a great college.

As for me, the only cost I incurred upon my parents while in high school, was my bus fare. I was admitted into Whitney M. Young High school, a school in a slum, which later turned out to be one of the finest schools in the city. My first day in school had me excited because I journeyed for over an hour to get to school. I expected a lot from my new school, and Whitney Young was no disappointment. It was as perfect as I'd imagined it to be, structure-wise. There were, however, tons of kids at Whitney Young, and I feared that most of them would be much older than I was. As a high school student, I always wondered if I was good enough. Only a few kids from my neighborhood attended Whitney Young. My classmate, Chiaka, was one of those few. We would ride the bus to school together on some mornings, as well as back home in the evening. Such was not the case in school though, as we were usually about our different, individual businesses. This was also the first time I'd be away with Craig's protection. And for once, I had to learn to ground myself. Day in, day out, I was consumed with the fear of not being enough. I saw the other kids as smart and always wondered if I measured, or would ever measure up to them.

As I rode the bus to school every day, I realized that Chicago was much bigger than I ever imagined it to be. As a student, I was focused on observing as much as I could to settle down as comfortably as possible into the new environment I found myself. Being exposed to kids from other parts of the country, I had to sort out my place in this school gradually. My mates discussed things such as the African-American elite, and a social club called Jack and Jill, through which most of them seemed to know each other, and all of which was very strange to me. This was the world I found myself in. It was not as though there were no kids from humble backgrounds like mine, yet, the mere exposure into the world of the rich helped me see something I had never, ever noticed- what they enjoyed thanks to privilege and connection, and the ease with which the rich got things done, because they knew those that mattered.

We wrote our first round of exams, and my grades were not bad, likewise the second. With each passing year, I regained the same kind of confidence I had back at Bryn Mawr. Gradually, my doubts disappeared, and I began to like my teachers. I loved my writing subjects but hated those that had to do with figures. I was not the best student, but I maintained a good academic record. At this time, Craig was a student at Princeton University. We missed him at home and felt his absence tremendously. Tons of big universities offered to recruit him but my parents insisted that he go to Princeton University because he had greater prospects there than anywhere else.

I hardly saw my parents during this period, as school activities took up most of my time. I knew that my parents were sacrificing a lot paying for college. Hence, I made up my mind not to burden them with anything extra. One of these days, my French teacher announced an excursion to Paris. Aware that it wasn't compulsory, I did not even mention it at home. Somehow, my parents got to find out and were puzzled as to why I had kept it away from them. Opening up, I told them it was too much money, but they asked that they be the judge of that. A few weeks later, I was aboard a plane with some of my classmates on a trip to Paris. My parents had never had a vacation in Europe, owned no house nor wealth, yet they were giving up everything for Craig and me.

It was time for college, and my new friend, Santita and I picked interest in schools on the East Coast. Santita's dad was a famous man, a Baptist preacher and a powerful political leader. Santita was interested in Harvard University. However, she was heartbroken when she visited Harvard, and was judged by her father's political actions, and not as an individual of her own. Around this time, I visited Craig in Princeton and spent a whole week with him. Shortly afterward, I began considering Princeton for college. Soon after, I got a letter offering me admission to come study at Princeton University.

CHAPTER 6

Key Takeaways

- *David and I split up.*
- *A new chapter begins.*
- *I begin running an after school program for kids.*

I arrived at Princeton University in 1981 in the company of my father, who personally drove me down to school. It wasn't just my dad and me though, I also had my boyfriend, David, tag along. There was an orientation program intended for first-year students, to enable them to settle into school with ease. While I wondered how this was of any help to most students, I figured I'd go, after all, Craig had attended the same program two years back. I was eager to leave town mainly because I had spent the last few months at a boring job at the bookbinding factory, which always reminded me of the need to go to college. David and I worked together, as his mom got both of us our jobs there. David attended college out of Chicago but came over during the holiday and summer breaks. He was a perfect gentleman, who found it pretty easy to bond with my family members.

I almost couldn't wait to alight from the car and get on with school already. There was a challenge, however: David! The minute we left Chicago, his demeanor had changed, and he began to look downcast. While I got my luggage out of my dad's car, I could already sense that he felt lonely. David and I had said we loved one another, but ours was a love that did not transcend beyond our immediate environments. At that moment, it dawned on us both that we had never sat to discuss this day, and were not entirely clear as to whether or not this was a temporary break, or perhaps, a complete breakup. I wanted something like what my parents had — real, true love. In a split second, I realized that David was not the man I shared all of those with. David and my dad left shortly afterward, and I never told him that was it, even though deep down within me, I knew.

I had a whole lot to learn about life on the Princeton Campus. Princeton was home to more whites than blacks and had a lot of male students. I felt uncomfortable initially, but soon enough, I began to adapt to my new environment. And unlike the way things were back at home, at Princeton, the only thing I needed to be attentive to was my academics; every other thing was provided adequately for our comfort as students. Nevertheless, I had to learn a whole new set of vocabulary. Concepts such as precepts and reading period were strange to me. There was only one lead I had available, and that was the fact that I was Craig's sister. As a top player on the University's basketball team, he had managed to whip a life around himself. Subtly, I eased my way into that life, getting to know his teammates and his friends.

For some reason, I imagined that the management of the University hated that black students stuck together as opposed to the composite, harmonic bonding they expected. This was not the case in Princeton, as I needed my black friends. We stood for and by each other, especially in situations where the white students outnumbered us.

I got a good, well-paying job as a work-study student. I worked as an assistant to the director of the TWC, helping out about ten hours of the week when I had no classes to attend. I loved my job; I was satisfied with my job. Above these, however, I liked my boss, Czerny

Brasuell. She was a sweet young lady who saw something worth nurturing in me. She was determined to bring out the best in me, constantly asking questions to challenge or spur my interest in certain subjects.

One day, Czerny asked if I had thought about running an after-school program for kids. Of course, I had not. Of late, I spent time with her son, Jonathan, but that was as far as it went. Besides, she paid me for my time, so I never really did consider setting up a program. But before I could even blink, I was in charge of three to four kids, several afternoons a week. We would all eat, play, do homework and get drained. For years, I had played with my dolls, and now I was doing it for real, tending to children.

Once every week, I would call home. Sometimes my father picked up, but my mother did the picking up most of the time. I would update them about what was happening in school, while they would feed my ears with happenings from home. My father always told me about everyone else's troubles, but never mentioned his, as though he had no worries. Not too long afterward however, I got to see the reality that I found so difficult to accept. Craig had a game, and my family drove down to see him play, and there, I saw my father reluctantly get into a wheelchair, allowing my mother to wheel him in. I couldn't bear it. He never wanted us to discuss his health, always claiming to be okay. Instead, he would ask if I was comfortable, and if I needed anything, to which I'd always reply in the negative.

CHAPTER 7

Key Takeaways
- *Home- farther than ever.*
- *Aunt Robbie passes on, and so does my grandfather.*
- *Life goes on!*

I gradually began to lose touch with my home-front. As the days passed, it grew more and more distant. As a college student, I had managed to keep in touch with a few friends from high school, Santita, most especially. I was doing great with my discipline, sociology. I started dating again, this time around, a footballer.

I was from two worlds, one could say; born in one, living in another. Whenever anyone asked where I was from, I was quick to say 'Chicago' adding with a tint of pride, for reasons that I'm yet to understand, 'the South Side.' I felt the need to correct the misrepresentation that had gone on for so long and to show the world that just like everyone else, I deserved a place at Princeton.

Princeton wasn't entirely 'away from home' for us. I did have an aunt who resided in Princeton, somewhere on the edge of town. Occasionally, she invited Craig and me over for dinner. She was a well-mannered, simple, polite old lady who hardly said anything of significance to us. Her food was however exactly what we always needed, having grown tired of dining hall food all year long.

Kevin, my footballer boyfriend, was from Ohio. Tall, sweet and rugged, he was in the same set as my brother. One day, he asked that we go driving, after which he parked in an open field and beckoned on me to come down. Before I knew it, we were running from one end to another. I was shocked when Kevin decided he'd put medical school aside and instead, pick up a career in becoming a sports mascot.

Suddenly, everyone I loved began to pass. First, it was my great-aunt, Robbie, followed by my grandfather. We all were hurt, but we had to move on. Spring came, and as was the custom, recruiters were on ground to arm their firms with the best of the graduating seniors. While all of these were going on, I was busy, focused on achieving my already set goals.

Now that I think about it, I realize that I was burned out in school. All through that time, I concentrated all of my energy into writing exams, theses, applying to law school and the rest. I was pretty good at arguing and I gradually convinced myself that I was 'law-worthy.' I never fully realized, however, that I placed so much premise on what people said, as opposed to what I truly wanted for myself. Deep down within me, I did whatever I did to get the approval of those I felt mattered.

But what happens after all of these? You keep reaching for more in a bid to satisfy peoples' expectations of you, that you gradually let who you are slip away.

CHAPTER 8

Key Takeaways

- *My job, my pride.*
- *Barack Obama: passionate and unconventional*
- *A love story begins.*

My office was on the forty-seventh floor, and this day, I was waiting patiently for Barack Obama to arrive. I was a busy, young lawyer, who avoided interaction of any sort. A couple of times, I played with my assistant, Lorraine, but for the most part, I was occupied with work.

I had a great office, beautiful enough to spend some time away from the hustle-bustle of the real world. I was well-paid at Sidley, and I did myself some good by stashing away money to pay for housing. Up until this point, I lived with my parents who had moved downstairs into my great-aunt Robbie, and her husband, Terry's apartment, downstairs, allowing me to take over our entire apartment. I had made some changes to in it to suit myself, but I was still content to come in through the kitchen door downstairs, as a means of dropping by to see my parents each day. I gave them quite a little amount of money that I know barely did anything, yet they always made it seem like a huge deal.

Back at work, I asked my assistant Lorraine, if she had any word about Barack, to which she replied in the negative. I was upset because I could not bear lateness. Barack Obama had just left law school, and usually, we would not hire first-year students for summer positions. His case was pretty different though, as word had spread that he was about the smartest lawyer we might have ever come across. Some even went as far as saying that not only was he brilliant, but that he was also cute.

I was unconvinced, trust me. And after another ten minutes, he finally arrived, apologizing for his lateness. I took him to my office, showed him what he needed to know, and finally handed him over to the senior partner with whom he'd be working all summer. Later that day, we had lunch together at a restaurant in the office building. I had a responsibility to make him happy, comfortable and to offer advice whenever he needed one, as it concerned the job. Shortly, however,

I realized that he wouldn't need any advice from me. He was about three years older than I was, and was more experienced than I'd ever been. I noticed something too. He was very confident about the path he had chosen for his life and career. He shared his life with me, and we both laughed as we talked about our backgrounds. And although I was initially unconvinced about him, I had to admit that he was not only intelligent but also highly passionate and unconventional.

The next few weeks saw us relating more often as Barack would usually drop by and find himself a seat in my office. We found it easy to connect with each other, perhaps because we shared similar mindsets. He was different from the previous summer associate I had, and it was not long before his status in the firm began to grow, and his inputs were often sought after. I had learned a lot about Barack in the past few weeks, but something struck me most importantly. He was single, and I thought I could fix that. I had tons of friends in Chicago, but I had very little interest in anyone from the opposite sex.

One evening, I took Barack to a bar with me, a place where I often met up with my friends. Being a fine, athletic, young man, I was certain anyone would be pleased to have him. Shortly after we arrived, he was neck deep in a conversation with my colleague in the finance department. Satisfied with myself, I got a drink and moved on with those I knew in the crowd. A few minutes later, he cast a glance at me, asking to be set free from the conversation, which was being dominated by the woman. I did not anyway, as I concluded that he was brave enough to do that himself.

As a child, my parents smoked. Craig and I hated it though, and we were not afraid to express our displeasure. We taught our parents about the harmful effects of smoking, although it took a while before they finally did quit smoking. And like my parents did back in the days, Barack smoked. He knew my stance on smoking, and I was appalled that someone as smart as Barack would be caught with such a dumb habit. He said nothing to me, merely acknowledging with a shrug that I was right. I had to admit however that things were changing between us, as specks of affection were fast forming in our hearts. We hung out soon after and had our first kiss. With that, things began to take shape, and everything started to feel as clear as day.

PART II: BECOMING US
CHAPTER 9
Key Takeaways
- *Love blossoms!*

The minute I allowed myself relax and enjoy the warmth of Barack's love, all my emotions came at me in top gear. He was to return to school at Harvard in a month, so we skipped the casual part of our relationship. Soon after, I began spending nights at his place, as I could not bear to have him with me, under the same roof as my parents.

Barack was very different from the other guys I had dated in the past. He enthralled me. I felt good, calm and secure with him. He was never about buying material things, but instead spent his funds purchasing different kinds of books. We still spent most of our time at work though. I insisted that our relationship is kept out of the public glare, particularly from our colleagues at work. This hardly worked anyway, because each time

Barack came by my office, Lorraine would give him a smile that said she knew something was up between us. Work, at this point, merely served as a distraction from our 'us' time, which we dearly longed for and couldn't wait to return to after working hours. Every day, I discovered something new about us — our similarities, differences and so much more. Barack loved the way I was raised, which was very different from his. And although I cannot remember having introduced Barack to my family that summer, my brother, Craig who was visiting at the time, said I did. My dad took a liking to Barack instantly, although deep down within himself, he had come to believe that like my first two boyfriends, Barack would soon be history.

Barack had spent tons of years trying to make sense of what his life was. His mother, Ann Dunham, had him at age 17, for a Kenyan man named Barack Obama. As fate would have it, the man was already married back home in Kenya. Following their divorce, Ann remarried a Javanese named Lolo Soetoro and moved to Jakarta, along with my Barack, who was about six years old at the time. He was happy in Indonesia and got on well with his stepfather.

Ever-willing to lend a helping hand, I was awestruck as I journeyed with him when a friend asked if he could lead a training event at a black parish on the South Side. Barack was more than excited to return to his old job. People sized him up as he walked through them, wondering who he was. Gently, he hung his jacket and was soon neck deep in a conversation that lasted about an hour, where he asked the people to speak up and share their opinions, needs, and experiences in the neighborhood. As they did, he also shared his story, explaining how we are all connected by our stories, and how possible it was to find in our individual stories, something worth converting into something useful.

He was not bothered by skepticism. He presented his idea, as difficult and impossible as it seemed, assuring them that it was possible to achieve their desire if they were willing to work at it. It was a matter of time before people bought into his opinion, convinced that together they could make this work.

Just before he returned to law school, he spilled the beans and said he loved me. And I knew it, for I loved him too. One thing we'd have to contend with was distance. Harvard was more than nine hundred miles away from Chicago, and he still had two years to go as a student, although he hoped to settle in Chicago when he was done schooling. We had no option now than to make good use of the phone, which at the time, was relatively new technology. He preferred to write letters, but I wasn't going to settle for postal services. And I made my point as clear as possible. And that was it; he became accustomed to using the phone. We spoke as much as we could, and our feelings remained intact.

It was not long after I got a call from Suzanne. I had called her earlier to tell of my relationship with Barack, and she sounded more excited than even I did. But this time around, things were different. She had cancer, and so did her mom. Weeks passed, and her mom died. Knowing the severity of things, I got a plane ticket and boarded a taxi to the hospital. Suzanne was in a coma, looking as beautiful as she always had. I began to wonder why Suzanne, of all people, at 26 would be in such a state. I was lost in thoughts when we realized that her breathing had grown ragged. And that was it. Suzanne passed on, leaving me with my Barack, my fancy job, and my life. And in that split second, I realized that life would go on, with or without you!

CHAPTER 10

Key Takeaways

- *Purpose-driven life!*
- *Papa dies!*

I began to journal that summer. I was not much of a writer, and so, my journal entries were occasional. Barack came back to Chicago over his summer break, and this time around, he spent the entire summer in my apartment. As a couple, we were learning to cohabit. Also, Barack was getting to know my family more personally. He had just accepted a job with a firm downtown, but he was not spending a lot of time in Chicago. He had also just been made the president of the Harvard law review for the coming year. Also, Barack was the first African-American to be selected in the publication's 103- year history, so huge a feat that it had earned him a feature in the New York Times. Barack was a big deal and could have gotten a big salary paying job. He was however uninterested in that, or the many other options people provided. He simply wanted to live in Chicago, write a book and find a job that was in tune with his values. Of course, this would mean deviating from the path of corporate law.

Barack stirred in me the need for a purpose-driven life. Every day with him made me feel entirely lost in this world, as though I had no sense of direction for my existence. It was for this reason that I began to journal. I realized as time went by that I had to admit the sad truth; I hated law, even if I was good at it. Secondly, I was deeply in love with a man whose ambition and intellect could gobble mine up. And although that was not his intention, I realized the need to get myself standing strong. This meant that I would have to find something I was passionate about, and in that haze, I had no idea what that was. I continued to practice law, while searching for something to satisfy my heart cry. I had just returned from a trip, and my mother came to pick me up from the airport. She noticed my mood, and there and then, as we drove home, I told her exactly how I felt about my job, or the profession I chose for myself. I also told her about my fears about what would happen to my finances if I left my job, still stressing the fact that I was not fulfilled within myself with what I presently did. I know this must have hit her hard, for she took a job only to be able to help out with paying my college fees. And for the first time, she didn't hide her displeasure, as she told me to make money first, before worrying about my happiness.

Quietly, I spent the next couple of months trying to improve myself. My dad's condition got worse, although, as always, he insisted he was fine. He did not lose his jovial sense of humor. Craig came by once in a while, along with his wife, Janis, to have dinner with us. Like me, my brother was unsatisfied with his job, despite the number of successes he had recorded. When it was time to leave, he would ask my father about his health, and once again he'd reply that he was fine. But we all saw it. His health was gradually failing, and it took more time than before to make minimal movements. In addition to his feet, something seemed to be swelling in his neck, causing a rattle in his voice. Despite these, my father refused to visit the hospital, insisting that doctors only brought bad news. We had all had enough. I told my father straight up that he owed it to us all to get medical help. Reluctantly, he agreed to go if I made the appointment myself. Relieved that we had everything under control, I was shocked when I came downstairs the next day, only to see my father dressed in work clothes, insisting that he no longer had to see the doctor and that he was perfectly fine.

Barack and I had toyed with the idea of marriage for the past couple of months. He was due to finish from Harvard, and would soon be back to pick up a job. As the months rolled by, we had discussed our views on marriage, and I was worried because we had very contrasting views. I wanted to get married; I had always wanted to. Barack was not against marriage, but at the same time, he was content with the life we lived, crazily in love with each other. I figured we'd work this out when Barack finally came around.

I booked an appointment for my father, with the doctor. However, it was my mother who got him there, in an ambulance. His feet had become badly swollen, and he had to admit it was painful walking on them. He was taken to the hospital at the University of Chicago. At this time, other parts of his body had also begun to swell. His endocrine system was barely under control anymore, and my father explained to the doctor that he had no idea how he missed this or that, as though there were not enough symptoms all the while he had been officially diagnosed with Cushing's syndrome. Day after day, we took turns to visit my dad in the hospital, spending as much time as we could with him. He could barely speak now, and we often decided to brighten him by calling him back with old memories.

One evening, I dropped by at the hospital, and the hallways station was rather quiet. My father was alone, as my mother had gone home for the night. My father who was only fifty-five was already looking like an old man. He was awake, but he was unable to speak to me. He held my hands in his and kissed them gently. I cried, knowing that we were at the end of the road and that my father was not going to recover. Once more, he kissed my hands, his way of telling me he loved me deeply, and that he was sorry for not having gone to the hospital earlier. I remained with him till he fell asleep that night, watching him struggling to breathe. I left the hospital that night, and drove home to meet my mother, alone, at home, to continue the rest of our lives; because, by morning, my father had died. He had a heart attack and passed on that night, leaving us everything he had ever owned.

CHAPTER 11

Key Takeaways

- *The pain of loss is great!*
- *Discovering myself.*
- *Barack proposes.*

Losing a loved one is painful. Very painful. The day after my dad died, Craig, my mom and I went to make funeral arrangements. While there, Craig and I got into a fight, our first and only fight as adult siblings. For some reason, I wanted my father to be buried in the most expensive casket available, while Craig opposed this strongly, saying that my father would prefer he be buried in something modest. The argument which started quietly soon exploded, while the funeral director pretended not to hear us. Grief-stricken, my mother stared at us in utter disbelief. Finally, Craig and I settled for something in between- not too plain, not too elaborate.

Later that day, we drove our mom back home. We all sat downstairs, overcome by grief. We broke out in tears for a long time, and only stopped when we were exhausted. However, at some point, it dawned on us all that my late father had shown us all who we were and how best to live, and at that moment, as difficult as it was, we all shared a laugh.

With my father's passing, I knew undoubtedly that life was short, and that I had a lot more to offer the world than stacks of legal briefs. I decided it was time to make a move. Unsure of what move to make, I sent letters of introduction to people and firms all around Chicago, writing directly to their legal departments. It's not as if I wanted a legal job anymore; it was only because I figured they'd most likely respond to my emails. A number of them did. I continually asked questions that would steer me on the right path, as I was clueless as to what I wanted to do.

One day, I visited Art Sussman's office, at the University of Chicago. My mom once worked for him as a secretary. He was shocked to discover that I never visited my mom at work. I never had a reason even to visit the university campus. At that point, it struck me that I'd have made an outstanding student of the University of Chicago if the divide hadn't been so pronounced. Having seen my resume, he told me to talk to Susan Sher. Susan was about 15 years older than I was. She again passed my resume to Valerie Jarrett, describing her as the person I needed to meet. Valerie had spared me twenty minutes out of her busy schedule. As we spoke, I realized she was someone to learn from. Right there, she offered me a job, but the salary was half of what I was earning. She advised that I take some time to think about whether or not I was prepared to make this sort of change. She called a few days later to follow up, and I merely told her I was still thinking about it. Just then, I asked the strangest question: if I could introduce her to my fiancé.

Barack came back to Chicago to spend time with me before returning to Harvard to finish up. Upon graduating, he returned to Chicago, right into my arms. I loved and felt loved by him. We had time to ourselves again, as a couple. He was excited at the thought of being done with school, especially as it availed him the opportunity to do whatever he found fulfilling. He had plenty of job options at his fingertips, and he was considering taking up an offer at Davis, Miner, Barnhill, and Galland. He saw opportunities as never-ending, unbothered by whether they'd remain so or will eventually dry up. Barack was a very trusting person, believing and keeping the faith alive when every other person had lost hope. He simply felt that if you stuck to doing things the way you thought you should, things were bound to fall in place. With his voice in my head, I knew he was encouraging me to go for it and make the change I dreaded so much.

It was not long after before Barack proposed to me. This was closely followed by my acceptance of the job offered by Valerie. Soon after, we decided to take a trip to Kenya where I got to meet with his half-sister and grandmother. At first, it felt out of place, but soon enough, I settled in. I knew I was out of my world, yet I was excited at the new world I had been launched into.

CHAPTER 12

Key Takeaways

- *Our marriage? Everything I'd ever dreamt of.*
- *Project VOTE!*

Barack and I got married in October 1992. Our wedding was a huge one, as we decided that if it was to hold in Chicago, then there was no use trimming the list. I had a very extended family, and I was not ready to leave any of them out on my big day. My friend, Santita was my maid of honor. Our wedding had most of our family members from far and near present; they swarmed us with their love. My mom looked at me from where she sat, with pride in her eyes. Barack stared at me, bright-eyed, with all the love in the world.

Our wedding song was a Stevie Wonder song titled 'We can conquer the world' which I first heard when I was a kid. My late grandfather had given me the album as a child and allowed me to play it whenever I came around. Barack, who wasn't so neck-deep into the whole marriage thing had been so sweet, even up until this point. He had been fully involved in every preparation towards the wedding, as much as I was.

Santita sang our wedding song, accompanied by the pianist. As a child, I could only imagine love, and who my 'you' would be. Yet, here we were, getting married.

Our wedding was held at the Trinity church and officiated by its Pastor. He welcomed all our family and friends and spoke about how glad he was to be uniting us in the presence of such a caring and loving community. At that point, the significance of the whole event dawned on me. And once again, within myself, I resolved that whatever the future held for us both, we were going into it, together.

Honeymoon came, and we traveled to San Francisco, spent some time in Napa and drove down Highway 1 to do a couple of strange stuff. The year had been pretty exhausting, yet we were ready to start strong, again. Barack, whom I thought would be busy working on his book, had to put the project on hold, while he attended to a job by a national, nonpartisan organization called Project VOTE! The pay was rather awful, yet because it was in tune with Barack's values, he threw himself into the job. I, on the other hand, had spent a year working with Valerie, acting as a connection to several departments in the city. As the days rolled by, I realized that government issues were broad and never seemed to have an end. I was also learning, from Susan and Valerie, to be unafraid of my voice, and never to second-guess the power in my point of view. Most importantly, I learned from both of them how to be a working mom, who balanced both her job and the home front comfortably well.

Barack and I returned from our honeymoon to receive both good and bad tales. The good news was that Bill Clinton won the November election and that Project VOTE! had registered over a hundred thousand voters, directly. The bad news was that Barack had very little time to finish up his book, and had decided to rent a cabin, away from the everyday distraction, so that he could complete the book in a couple of weeks. Then came the shocker! His mother had rented him the perfect cabin in Sanur... nine thousand miles away from me.

Sadly, he flew to Bali and spent five solid weeks on his own while working on his book, "Dreams from my father." Meanwhile, I remained in my house in Euclid Avenue, trying to drain out my loneliness by meeting up with friends and having workout sessions in the evenings. Sometimes, I'd find myself saying 'my husband' which was somewhat new and unusual, but nice.

Soon after, Barack returned home, having completed the book. In a matter of months, his agent sold the book to a new publisher, paying off his debt as well as securing a plan for publication. However, what mattered the most to me was that I had him back to myself, and we were fast returning to our life as newlyweds. Months went by, and soon enough, we were able to buy ourselves a condo. I also switched jobs, leaving Susan and Valerie as I plunged into the kind of non-profit job I had always longed for. There was still a lot I was yet to figure out, but I was content being happy. And for me, happy was all I needed to be.

CHAPTER 13

Key Takeaways
- *Success or failure lay in my hands.*
- *Barack gets into politics!*
- *Baby Malia is born.*

I was pretty tense at my new job. A brand new organization called the Public Allies had just started its Chicago Chapter, and I was hired to be the executive director. It was pretty much a new firm in a new firm, and I had no professional experience to lend to the job. Still, I took it on wholeheartedly, determined to give my best. There was a challenge, however, regarding pay. Non-profit firms do not pay. Initially, I was offered a very small salary, way below what I earned while I worked with Susan and Valerie. I could not afford to say yes to such an amount, having loans to pay off and a husband who had law school loans to offset. When I mentioned how much debt was hanging on me as a result of schooling, the management found it hard to believe. Eventually, however, they went out and got new funding to have me come on board.

With that in place, I went on about my job, putting in all I had. I began by getting an office, loads of second-hand chairs and a ton of other useful things. Next up, I started to leverage every contact I had in Chicago, seeking donors and people who could support us. I realized mainly that the success or failure of Allies depended on me. What excited me the most was finding the Allies. We placed adverts everywhere that mattered, visited community colleges and schools, went to community meetings and so much more. By fall, we had twenty-seven Allies working around Chicago. They were a group of high spirited, diverse individuals, idealistic and realistic in their thinking. Every Friday, they all gathered to examine, connect, and go through a series of professional development workshops. More than anything, I loved and looked forward to these Fridays. I enjoyed walking them through any challenges they might have had. If I heard negative reports about any of them, I was firm in letting them know what was expected.

The way I tended to Public Allies was pretty much the same way anyone would manage a new baby. I frequently bothered about what had been done and what had to be done, marking and crossing my checklists. Soon after we graduated our first class of 27 allies, a new batch of 40 emerged, and we continued to grow from there on. At that point in my life, I felt that I was making an impact, giving back to society. I was able to understand now how my husband felt with the success of Project VOTE!

All this while I settled into Public Allies, Barack was teaching a class on racism and the law at the University of Chicago, while working by day at his law firm. He managed to find a balance between teaching, lawyering, and organizing. When Barack returned from Bali, he had spent more than a year writing the second draft of his book. He liked to work from a small space in the house which I fondly referred to as a 'hole.' I had come to know that someone like Barack always needs a hole, where he could do all of his study and reading without intrusion. That was his way of refueling, I guess. We, therefore, made it a point of note always to have a 'hole' wherever we moved, even if we were just on vacation. His book, "Dreams From My Father" finally got published in 1995, and although it got great reviews, it only sold modestly. That was okay, however. Somehow, in that book, he had managed to put the pieces of his life together.

Barack's mom had suddenly been diagnosed with ovarian cancer. As far as we knew, his half-sisters were there to look after her, and so she was in good hands. Still, getting to hear the news when his mother's cancer was at an advanced stage left Barack in deep thoughts. In Chicago, it was time for elections again. A popular senator, Alice Palmer was contesting for the position of a Democratic contender in the state's Second District, leaving her senatorial position open. This opened up the possibility that Barack could run for it. He asked me, and at first, I was skeptical. Finally, however, I gave in, giving him all the support he needed.

Shortly after he announced his intention to run, his mother passed away. Barack was in so many ways like his mother, who was always ready to embrace the unfamiliar. Her condition deteriorated so quickly that Barack couldn't even get to say goodbye. He was in severe pain, as the loss of his mother cut through him so profoundly.

Barrack got into politics, and as a good person, he was bent on impacting the world. With the legislature in session, we got to see only a few days during the week.

To make up for this, we would meet up every Friday to have dinner at a restaurant called Zinfandel.

I was thirty-two years old now, and I was not pregnant. It was beginning to get frustrating. Barack and I tried so hard, yet we couldn't come up with a pregnancy. A while later, I got pregnant, but I had a miscarriage that crushed my hopes of motherhood. Miscarriages are about one of the most hurtful experiences in a woman's life. Barack and I ran a series of tests which all revealed that both of us were perfectly fine. After what seemed like a decade, we decided to go through with an IVF. It was successful, and soon enough, I got pregnant. On July 4, 1998, we welcomed Malia Ann Obama into this world.

CHAPTER 14

Key Takeaways

- *Motherhood- an experience of a lifetime.*
- *Barack faces political troubles.*
- *Natasha is born!*

Birthing Malia was one of the best things to happen to me, ever. And I wasted no time getting used to being a mother. Motherhood suddenly began to control all of my actions and decisions. Barack and I studied our bundle of joy, as though we could hear her through her tiny, little giggles. As new parents, we were pretty obsessed with our baby, often laughing at what parenthood had done to us both.

Months after Malia's birth, I returned to work at the University of Chicago, on a part-time basis. I was trying to be the perfect mother and career woman all at the same time. We already hired a babysitter, Glorina, to take care of Malia. Glorina, fondly called Glo, loved Malia deeply, and for me, that was more than enough.

I did not realize early enough that the idea of a part-time job was a trap. You would do all you usually would have done, in shorter hours and at half pay. I always felt a sense of guilt, because, for me, the part-time job which was meant to give me more freedom only got me doing all I usually should have done, in halves. Meanwhile, Barack was neck-deep in politics, as he had been reelected to a four-year term in the Senate. He was beginning to dream big, with thoughts of running for congress flooding his mind. I did not think it was a good idea at the time, especially since he was going to be running against Rush, a very popular politician. He, however, had so many advisers and supporters who encouraged him to run.

When Malia was almost 18 months old, we made a trip home to Hawaii at Christmas, so she could visit her great-grandmother, Toot, who was 77 years old at the time. We had cleared our tables to enable us to embark on the trip in time, only for Barack to ask for some more time as politics came in the way. I did not like this news, but I understood it was beyond his control. As far as I was concerned, as long as we made it to Hawaii, whenever that was, was fine by me.

Officially, my husband was running for Congress. This implied that Malia and I saw less and less of him at home. Eventually, we flew to Hawaii on the 23rd of

December. Malia loved the Waikiki Beach as she made her way through the shoreline, having fun. We had a beautiful Christmas with Toot. While there, Barack got a call concerning his intention to vote, demanding that he be back home in 48 hours or less for the crime-bill vote. Again, I was distraught, but understanding that it was politics, I had no choice but to agree as I watched him rebook our flights.

Out of the blues, the unexpected happened. Malia caught a fever, one so severe that even Tylenol did almost nothing. She also seemed to have been infected in one of her ears as she continually tugged at it. It dawned on us both that she could not fly in this state. Barack had a choice to make that night. He could return home, and we'd join him later. To my greatest surprise, he did not leave. Shortly after, I heard him place a call through to his legislative aide that day, explaining that he'd miss the crime-bill vote. We stayed back for a few more days, got our daughter treated and returned home to Chicago.

We met a different state of politics in Chicago when we went home, as the crime-bill vote had failed to pass the state legislature. It's not as though Barack's presence would have made any serious changes, yet, his opponents saw it as a reason to get at him, even though he explained why he was away. They wrote it all off saying he was holidaying and had decided not to return to vote on something so significant. The press didn't make it more comfortable as they continually churned out unprintable things about my husband. I was not used to any of these, and it hurt to think that a right decision had cost him so much.

Barack continued to campaign against all the odds. I could hear the agony in his voice when he spoke. The elections came, and he lost the Democratic primary to Bobby Rush.

Our second baby girl, Natasha, was born in 2001, after a single round of IVF. Barack and I were more than excited to have her. I loved being with my daughters; Malia was about three years old at the time, and about to start preschool.

While I was contemplating staying at home to focus on our girls, I received a call from Susan Sher, my former mentor, about the need to hire an executive director at the University of Chicago medical center, and that she thought I could give it a shot. I thought about it endlessly, and finally decided it was worth a try. I went for the interview with Natasha and even went as far as placing her on the table. I had come to know that there was no single formula to motherhood. I got the job, Barack had his two jobs, we had two cars and a condo. And despite his fallout from the elections, Barack still had ideas about trying for a higher office.

CHAPTER 15

Key Takeaways

- *In the period before Barack got into the Senate, my goals included normalcy and stability.*
- *Barack was invited by John Kerry to give the keynote address at the 2004 Democratic National Convention held in Boston.*
- *Barack got into the Senate and was the only black person there.*
- *After that feat, people began to tip him to make a run for president in the 2008 general elections.*

Even though Barack had other essential concerns to attend to, my major goals involved normalcy and stability. Barack had to be away for most of the time. I didn't like it, but I had to live with the fact that it was just a part of his job. I had stopped fighting it. With Barack ending the day in a faraway hotel, the girls and I ended ours in the shelter of home.

Part of the things on Barack's plate was campaigning for a seat in the U.S. Senate ahead of the fall 2004 elections. He was convinced that he could do more and better in Washington. We convened an informal meeting at Valerie Jarrett's house to see what some of our closest friends thought about the idea of a Senate run. Valerie had told me that she didn't support Barack's run for the Senate, however, Barack's smooth argument and response for every "but what about?" question we threw his way made so much sense.

At the 2004 Democratic National Convention held in Boston, Barack was invited by John Kerry to give the keynote address. Choosing him to speak to an audience of millions had been a huge gamble especially as he was a black man in what was historically a white man's business. Barack was not just a senator; he was the only black person in the Senate. People seemed to feel that he would make a run for president in 2008. Every reporter asked about it. Even Malia at six and a half wanted to know. It was all down to me in the end. A campaign for presidency would be costly. We would have to give up our time, togetherness, and even our privacy. I said yes because I firmly believed in Barack becoming a great president. I loved him and had faith in him although I didn't think he could win because after all, Barack was a black man in America.

CHAPTER 16

Key Takeaways

- *The primary contests for Barack's run for presidency began in Iowa.*
- *Barack ran an unusual campaign.*
- *Hilary Clinton was a major contender in the race.*
- *We made the declaration for presidency on February 10, 2007.*
- *A total of nine Democrats were in the race for presidency.*

Once we agreed to Barack being able to run, it was almost as though he had to be everywhere at once. When the primary contests started in Iowa, Barack had to hire staffs, woo donors who could write huge checks, and figure out how best to resonate with people while introducing his candidacy.

Barack knew he was an unusual candidate and so wanted to run an unusual campaign; one that listened to the voices of the unheard and disenfranchised. Hilary Clinton had declared her candidacy about a month earlier. A month before that, John Edwards had also launched his campaign speaking in front of a New

Orleans home that had been ravaged by Hurricane Katrina. A total of nine Democrats eventually entered into the competition.

February 10, 2007, was our announcement day. It was a beautiful midwinter Saturday morning. I wasn't a person who fancied spending her Saturday at a political rally. This was totally unlike anything I'd experienced before. Hilary Clinton proved to be a serious and formidable opponent. Every Democrat knew the Clintons were hungry for a win. One of Barack's most significant challenges was to woo long-standing black voters who were loyal to Bill Clinton to himself. As a black candidate, Barack couldn't afford to stumble in any way. We had to raise a whole lot of money and start spending it on the campaign fast. Our focus was hugely on Iowa which was mostly rural and had more than 90 percent of its inhabitant as whites.

The campaign taught us that each day was another race to be run. Barack's safety was also another important issue of which I didn't want to bother myself with. We grew up witnessing assassination attempts on the Kennedys, Martin Luther King Jr., John Lennon, and

Ronald Reagan. With Barack as a black man, the risk of him getting shot was not any lower.

CHAPTER 17

Key Takeaways

- *Barack was heavily scrutinized and monitored a few months to the general elections.*
- *He now had to win every American's support and not just that of Democrats.*
- *Barack needed the support of every state and territory.*
- *As much as we got more and more people encouraging us, we also saw an increase in haters.*

Just a few months to the general election, the buzz about Barack seemed to increase the more. People took note of how he spent every minute of the day, which states he visited the most, which diner he had his breakfast, and even what kind of meat he ordered to go along with his eggs. He was seriously watched, measured and evaluated. People wanted to know who the candidate was. Was he weak? Was he a snob? A phony? Was he a true American?

Barack's campaign had gone beyond winning the support of Democratic voters. He now had to win every American's heart. Hilary Clinton still constituted a challenging opposition as she and Barack had spent the winter and spring of 2008 competing for every state and territory to become the most preferred candidate. Other candidates had all dropped out by the end of January.

As the campaign intensified, we got more and more support. I got encouraging texts from Oprah Winfrey. Stevie Wonder, my childhood idol, showed up to play at campaign events. Barack's message of hope lifted us. And it was going to be a defining moment for the nation if a black man were elected as president. However, as Barack's popularity increased, so did his haters. There were people and investigators combing through every piece of his background looking for any incriminating material.

CHAPTER 18

Key Takeaways

- *I cast my vote for Barack on November 4, 2008.*
- *I made sure Malia and Sasha didn't miss school that day.*
- *The polls showed that Barack was on his way to winning.*
- *Barack prepared a victory speech as well as a speech for concession.*
- *By ten o'clock that night, Barack was announced as the forty-fourth president of the United States.*

On November 4, 2008, four months later, I cast my vote for Barack. We arrived at our polling place in the gym at Beulah Shoesmith Elementary School early that morning. I thought going to school was still a good idea even on Election Day. So I packed lunch boxes for Malia and Sasha, got them dressed and ready for school.

Voting for me was like a ritual as I had voted for Barack many times before in primaries and general elections, in state-level and national races, so this trip to the polls was no different. Election Day was symbolic of a leap that you've made but haven't landed. After months of everything going too fast, Barack and I hosted family and friends at home. Later on, he went out to settle his nerves with a difficult thrash-or-be-thrashed game of basketball.

The polls were revealing that Barack was poised to win. However, he had prepared two possible speeches for the night ahead - one for a victory and the other for a concession. My fingers began to get numb, and a nervous tingle ran through my body as the evening drew closer.

Barack had retreated upstairs needing a personal moment. He sat at his desk and looked over the text of his victory speech in the little book-strewn office adjacent to our bedroom. It was exactly ten o'clock when the news revealed pictures of my smiling husband who was to become the forty-fourth president of the United States. On the stage where we were to emerge as the new first family, over 200,000 people had gathered to greet us with many of them waving little American flags.

PART III: BECOMING MORE

CHAPTER 19

Key Takeaways

- *More than forty-three different women had taken the role of First Lady before me.*
- *I made sure to define myself and establish the kind of First Lady I wanted to be.*
- *We enrolled the girls in Sidwell Friends when we moved to Washington after our traditional Christmas holiday in Hawaii.*
- *Malia and Sasha learned to conduct themselves in a manner commendable of people who were being watched publicly.*

By the time I became the First Lady, more than forty-three different women had already occupied that seat. From Jackie Kennedy to Rosalynn Carter to Nancy Reagan to Hilary Clinton to Laura Bush, each one of them had done it in their unique way. By being the only African American First Lady to come to the White House, I knew from the onset that an entirely different standard would judge me.

Even though I knew I wasn't coming into a role that was a joyride, I was humbled and excited to be First Lady. I had used the seventy-six days between election and inauguration to establish the kind of First Lady I would want to be. I had learned from the campaign that public judgment sweeps in to fill any void if you do not go out and define yourself immediately. I was determined to make good on my promises of supporting military spouses and helping them share their stories, planting a garden and taking up the task to improve children's health and nutrition on a larger scale.

We moved to Washington after our traditional Christmas holiday in Hawaii so that Malia and Sasha could start school immediately after the winter break. We enrolled the girls at Sidwell Friends, a private Quaker school with an excellent reputation. On the first day of school, Barack had hoped to drive the girls all the way to school, but that was a bad idea. His motorcade was too big, and he had become too heavy. I could pick out the pain in his face from not being able to take the girls to school. Instead, my mother followed the girls to school in a black SUV with smoked windows made of bulletproof glass which would become their new form of a school bus.

Malia and Sasha quickly learned what it meant to be watched publicly. Throughout the inauguration, they conducted themselves perfectly, never fidgeting, slouching, or forgetting to smile. After the ceremony, they were grateful to heave a sigh of relief and release themselves from all the ceremonial dignity. We rode home in the limo with the girls blasting Beyoncé on the stereo just as if it were any old day. We were happy to be the First Family, but we were even happier to be ourselves still.

CHAPTER 20

Key Takeaways

- *I always imagined the White House to be a huge fancy hotel where you and your family are the only guests.*
- *I turned my dressing room into a place where I could read, work and watch TV all by myself.*
- *I made sure the girls continued to live a normal life by ensuring that they could play in the hallway and outside on the lawn.*
- *On assumption of the presidency, Barack's life became more orderly and he could show up for dinner on time.*

I have always told people who ask about life in the White House that it is like living in a fancy hotel where the only guests are you and your family. The building is of very high quality. With its thick walls and solid planking, sound in residence tends to get absorbed quickly. Also, the bomb-resistant glass in the windows is always kept shut for security reasons. The house staff makes sure that the place is sparkling clean. There are a lot of rooms, and they are all enormous. I converted my dressing room to my de facto private office. This room from which Laura Bush had shown me the Rose Garden view was where I could sit by myself to read, work, or watch TV.

Living in the White House changed a lot of things for us. As a child of the South Side, I had to adjust to rooms designed by a high-end interior decorator. My daughters also had the liberty of making a custom order for their breakfast from a chef. However, I made sure that I loosened some of the formalities and protocols in the place. I had our girls make their beds every morning, act polite and gracious, and live in such a way that they felt at home. They could play in the hallway or even outside on the South Lawn. After all, the girls and I were only enjoying these luxuries because of the position Barack held.

Barack was surrounded with a lot of attention and this kind of contradicted the fact that I didn't want the girls to think that it was normal for a household to revolve solely around the needs of the man. With fifty staffers on his mail, a six-person team in charge of his briefing books, and a handful of chefs and grocery shoppers concerned with his nutrition, Barack could ignore all home maintenance duties which were unappealing to him and focus on weightier matters.

Barack's life became more orderly than ever in his first month in office. He was able to show up for dinner on time; this was in contrast to life in Chicago where he was always far away in the Senate campaigning for a higher office. For me, I had to limit my circle of friends to a tiny one. Melissa, my deputy chief of staff, gave out her phone number and email address instead of mine. However, the girls had it easier because they were able to make new friends.

In the first months of office, I was very optimistic. However, this optimism was tempered by the politics of red-versus-blue. With Barack as president, he faced massive resistance from the Republicans who fought hard to thwart every of his effort to defeat the economic crisis. They disagreed to measures that would save or create millions of jobs and tried in every way possible to prove him wrong.

CHAPTER 21

Key Takeaways

- *Barack and I still had time together for dates.*

- *There were Secret Service agents who became our security detail and swore with their lives to protect us.*

- *Senator Ted Kennedy gave us the gift of a seven-month-old Portuguese water dog which we named Bo.*

- *I had to make significant changes in my fashion choices as the media became more interested in it.*

Our lives with Barack as president never fell short of the romantic activities we did. He kept good on his promise of date nights with me by taking me out on a date on one particular Saturday evening at the end of May. Just like date nights were a weekly sacred ritual in Chicago, we were continuing the tradition here. Even though we've had dinners in recent times, it was only limited to the ones we hosted and the performances we went to see at Kennedy Center. These events were always crowded with lots of other peoples, and we couldn't have our time together.

Barack had help picking a place where we would eat. The restaurant, which was close to Washington Square Park, was one I loved for their locally-grown foods specialty. New York had always been vast and awe-inspiring for me. However, I did feel a bit guilty as our presence in the city disrupted the peaceful and normal Saturday evening. Sitting at a table in a discreet corner of the restaurant didn't make us less evident to people. Anyone coming in had to be body checked with a magnetometer wand.

It was apparent that we needed this break from life at the White House. In spite of its comfort and beauty, it remains a fortress and is run in that manner. The Secret Service agents who swore with their lives to protect us usually preferred that we stay on the house grounds for safety reasons. We pushed all that behind us during our evening in New York. It was a magical atmosphere with candlelight conversations, food, and drink.

Barack and I never ran out of what to discuss. That night, we set aside the political and governance issues and focused more on issues bordering on our daughters, my mom. Sooner or later, Barack would tip his head and give that hearty laugh that I loved. We also talked about the latest addition to the family. Bo, a seven-month-old Portuguese water dog, was a gift from Senator Ted Kennedy. The girls played hide-and-seek with him on the South Lawn. They ran about as he followed their voices. Bo became an essential member of our family, and everyone loved him.

At a point in Barack's campaign, the media began to get more interested in what I was wearing. My flats, my pearls, my belts, my cardigans were all reported in the news. Fashion bloggers thrive on this, and they were out to get me late in the summer of 2009 at a family trip to the Grand Canyon. A photograph of me getting off Air Force One dressed in a pair of shorts seemed to them to portray a lack of dignity on my part. When Vogue proposed that I be on the cover page, I upped my game and chose my outfits which included dresses by Jason Wu and Narciso Rodriguez.

CHAPTER 22

Key Takeaways

- *Barack's calm leadership brought order to a lot of events.*
- *He cleared the public's doubts after he released pictures of him and Sasha splashing around in the waters of Florida after the BP oil spill.*
- *I visited Haiti with Jill Biden three months after the 2010 earthquake.*
- *In 2011, Barack mentioned Osama bin Laden to me for the first time.*
- *We took away most of the strict protocols of the White House by opening it up for more people, especially children.*

As First Lady, there were a lot of things that were beyond my control. Barack got blamed for many of these happenings even when he had no hold over them. However, his job was to take the storms of blames and transform it into calm leadership every week of the year. How Barack and I responded to the instability significantly affected a lot of things.

The local economies of the Gulf of Mexico suffered after the BP oil spill which made people unwilling to return there for vacation. So we took a family trip to Florida where Barack and Sasha took a swim and released photos of their fun time to the media. This went a long way to reassure the people that they too could trust the water.

When Jill Biden and I traveled to Haiti three months after the 2010 earthquake, it was to remind Americans not to turn their eyes away from the pain of others too quickly. We saw children who had lost everything, including their families, live life bubbling with hope by forging grief and resilience together.

I also tried as often as I could to visit military hospitals to see our American troops convalescing from the wounds of war. My first visit to Walter Reed National Military Medical Center ended up exceeding the ninety minutes I was scheduled to be there for into about four hours.

It wasn't until sometime early in 2011 that Barack mentioned Osama bin Laden. Bin Laden who was the world's most wanted man had evaded detection for years and capturing or killing him was among Barack's top priorities when he assumed office.

Beyond living inside the enclosure of the presidency for more than two years now, Barack and I ensured that our kids had a typical experience. We opened up the White House to more people, especially children, to reduce most of the strict formalities and traditions.

CHAPTER 23

Key Takeaways

- *Barack's year of re-election was in 2012.*

- *I made sure to show gratitude to the rich history I had to uphold by honoring those who were before me.*

- *The cost of reelection spiraled into over a billion dollars.*

- *Barack's approval rating plunged into its greatest depth with fears of a new recession.*

- *Election Day on November 6, 2012 saw us waving to the crowd from the stage again, glad that we had another four years.*

Barack's reelection year in 2012 got me thinking about the rich history that I was to uphold. This wasn't the history of presidents or First Ladies such as John Quincy Adams, Woodrow Wilson, Eleanor Roosevelt or Mamie Eisenhower. Instead, it was the struggles of people like Sojourner Truth, Harriet Tubman, Rosa Parks and Coretta Scott King that kept me on my feet. These women's lives along with my mother's and grandmother's lives were nothing compared to the one I now had. However, they went out of the way to ensure that I lived in a better world and I have no other way to show gratitude for this than to do life in a way that honored them.

I wasn't going to let them down, so I improved on how I made speeches, how I ran events, and how I pushed my policy advisers to spread out more in growing the reach of Let's Move and Joining Forces. The cost of the reelection was huge, and it was more stressful than the first. To keep our campaign competitive, we had to raise over a billion dollars.

Barack and I were very much optimistic about winning the election even though there was still that little fear of the possibility of losing. We never voiced it out. The stakes of the election were far too high. It would determine everything from the fate of the new healthcare law to whether America would be part of the global effort to combat climate change.

Barack went through a bruising period in the summer of 2011 with a group of obstinate congressional Republicans refusing to authorize the issuing of new government bonds. Also, many blamed Barack for the consistent but sluggish growth of jobs and the stunted progress the nation had in recovering from the 2008 crisis. Barack's approval rating improved and hit a two-year high following the death of Osama bin Laden. However, it all came crashing down to its lowest depths just a few months later with the events of the debt-ceiling brawl and worries about a new recession.

Election Day, November 6, 2012, brought with it the fears of waiting for an entire nation to accept or reject us. The campaign had significantly worn us out, and the polls were always showing that Barack had only a tenuous lead over Mitt Romney. Barack remained calm all through even though the pressure had made him skinnier than usual. During this period, he faced working on his campaign, governing the nation, while also responding to the events of a terrorist attack on American diplomats in Benghazi, Libya, and responding to Hurricane Sandy which swept in just a week before the election.

However, in the end, Barack would go on to all but one of the battleground states on election night. He'd own among the youth, minorities, and women, just like he did in 2008. After Mitt Romney called to concede we were immediately dressed up and waving from a stage ready for another four years.

CHAPTER 24

Key Takeaways

- *We made an exception to the security protocols and allowed Malia ride in her date's car on prom night.*
- *Malia finished her junior year at Sidwell in the spring of 2015.*
- *As the girls got older, we made their attendance at events at the White House optional.*
- *Donald Trump announced his candidacy for president early in the summer from his Trump Tower in Manhattan.*
- *Donald Trump succeeded Barack as the next president of the United States by winning the Electoral College.*

Giving Malia and Sasha a normal life was one of our biggest concerns as parents. In the spring of 2015, Malia was just finishing her junior year at Sidwell. She had been invited to prom by a boy she kind of liked. Even though she was becoming a little more adult every day, to us, she remained our mostly-enthusiastic little girl. For security reasons, Malia and Sasha were not allowed to ride in someone else's car, and even though

Malia had a provisional license which allowed her to drive around town on her own, there were always agents following in their vehicle. However, we were going to make an exception for prom night.

As her date arrived that evening, she asked us to play it cool. We shook the young man's hand, snapped a few pictures, and gave Malia a hug before sending them on their way. As parents, Barack and I often thought of how unfair it was for our daughters to carry an added responsibility based on who their father was. Both of us had been wild and done dumb things as teenagers without an entire nation watching us.

With time, Sasha and Malia soon outgrew many of the rituals at the White House. One of them was the pardoning of a live turkey just ahead of the Thanksgiving holiday. We then made their attendance at the pardon, as well as other events at the White House, entirely optional. We would later go on to enjoy a baseball game in Havana, walk along the Great Wall of China, and visit the Christ the Redeemer statue in Rio before Barack's presidency was over.

By the fall of 2015, it was time to move with the new winds of politics. The next presidential campaign had entered into full motion with the Republican side consisting of governors such as John Kasich and Chris Christie, and senators such as Ted Cruz and Marco Rubio, and more than a dozen others. Democrats, however, were faced with a choice between Hilary Clinton and Bernie Sanders. Donald Trump announced his candidacy early in the summer standing inside Trump Tower in Manhattan. I concluded that nothing in his character or campaign suggested that he was serious about his desire to govern.

In the end, Donald Trump turned out to be America's choice for president. I woke up to the news that he had been elected to succeed Barack as the next president of the United States. Hilary Clinton won nearly three million more votes than her opponent, but Trump swept the Electoral College. I only wished more people, especially women, turned out to vote rather than choose a misogynist as their new president. But there was nothing we could do about the result.

Made in the USA
Columbia, SC
02 January 2019